Who Lives Here?

Written by Sandra Iversen

Who lives in this log?
Is it a bug or a bat?

2

bug

log

3

Who lives in this den?
Is it a fox or an ox?

4

fox

den

5

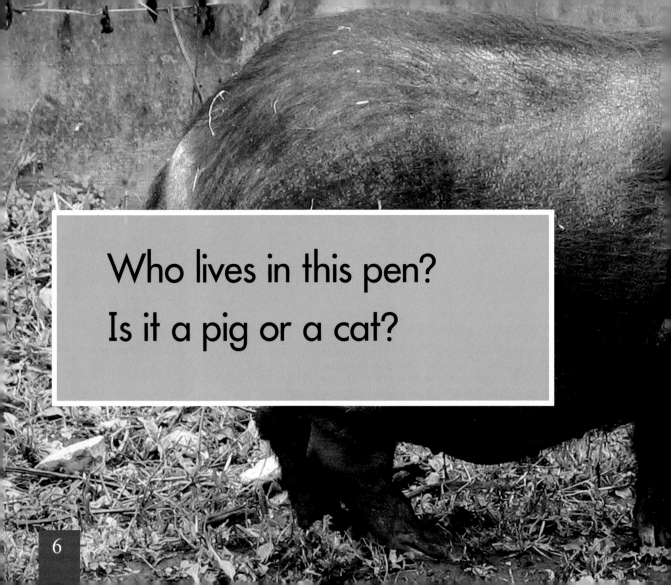

Who lives in this pen?
Is it a pig or a cat?

pig

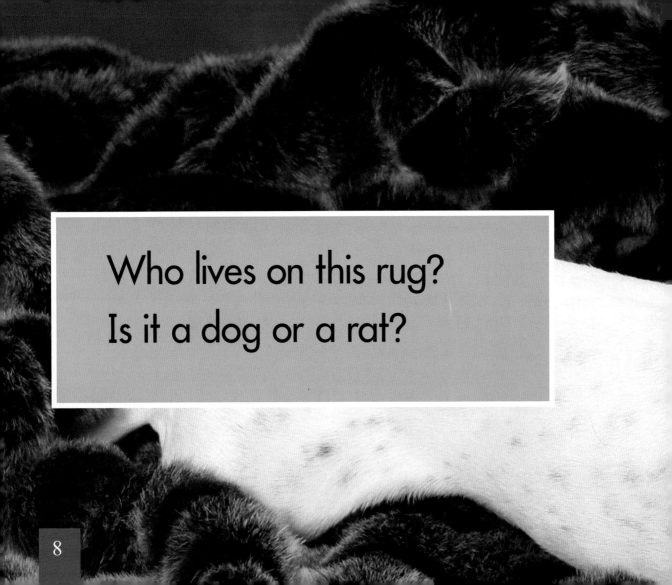

Who lives on this rug?
Is it a dog or a rat?

8

dog

rug

Who lives on this hill?
Is it a ram or a hen?

ram

11

Glossary

bug

dog

fox

pig

ram